For Daniel —
With best wishes –
Henry
Jan. 2021

AS THE CROW FLIES

POEMS

By

Henry Weinfield

DOS MADRES

2021

DOS MADRES PRESS INC.
P.O. Box 294, Loveland, Ohio 45140
www.dosmadres.com   editor@dosmadres.com

Dos Madres is dedicated to the belief that the small press is essential
to the vitality of contemporary literature as a carrier of the new voice,
as well as the older, sometimes forgotten voices of the past. And in an
ever more virtual world, to the creation of fine books pleasing to the
eye and hand.

Dos Madres is named in honor of Vera Murphy and Libbie Hughes,
the "Dos Madres" whose contributions have made this press possible.

Dos Madres Press, Inc. is an Ohio Not For Profit Corporation and a
501 (c) (3) qualified public charity. Contributions are tax deductible.

Executive Editor: Robert J. Murphy

Illustration & Book Design: Elizabeth H. Murphy
www.illusionstudios.net

Typeset in Adobe Garamond Pro & Cochin
ISBN 978-1-948017-84-8
Library of Congress Control Number: 2020936696

First Edition
Published by Dos Madres Press, Inc.

ACKNOWLEDGMENTS

I am grateful to the Institute for Scholarship in the Liberal Arts of the College of Arts and Letters at the University of Notre Dame for its generous support for this book.

I would also like to express gratitude to the editors of the publications in which some of these poems first appeared: *The Blue Lyra Review, Colorado Review, Hudson Review, Literary Imagination, Marsh Hawk Review*

"*L'Dor V'Dor*: Chant of the Jews of Michiana as They Contemplate the Past and the Future" was commissioned by the Michiana Jewish Historical Society for a book of photographs: *From Generation to Generation: The Jews of Michiana*. South Bend, IN: The Michiana Jewish Historical Society, 2014. 2-3.

"*Paradise Lost*: A Poem in Twelve Books: The Shorter Version" was commissioned by The Milton Society of America and published in the *Newsletter of the Milton Society of America* (2016).

The three "Academic Addresses" were delivered on various occasions to students and faculty of the Program of Liberal Studies at the University of Notre Dame.

TABLE OF CONTENTS

ᐧ I ᐧ

THE IRONIES

· I ·

THE IRONIES

THE IRONIES

What was it that you thought you had to say?
—Though possibly you said it anyway:
It turned out to be different than you thought.

What was it that you thought you'd come to know,
So long ago you can't remember now?
It turned out to be different than you thought.

What was it that you thought that you would be—
When you had come into maturity?
It turned out to be different than you thought.

▾　　▾　　▾

It turned out to be different than you thought,
Different from everything that you were taught.
You couldn't ever have imagined it.

The things that you evaded or forgot
Were details deeply woven in the plot.
You couldn't ever have imagined it.

Whatever you intended came to naught
Or turned out to be different than you thought.
You couldn't ever have imagined it.

▾　　▾　　▾

You couldn't have imagined that the doors
You opened closed off others that were yours,
Or that the forms revealed themselves as veiled.

It didn't seem impossible to seize
The golden apples of the Hesperides—
Where the eternal verities prevailed.

Like everyone you wanted everything
(The autumn simultaneous with the spring)—
For which no kind of medicine availed.

THE VALE OF DISENCHANTMENT

Vale, dark vale, we dwell within the Vale
Of Disenchantment, having torn the veil
Enveloping the things we couldn't see.

The things we couldn't see we now see well—
In this dark vale, unveiled, in which we dwell
In disenchantment—will not let us be.

They will not let us be, but work their will;
And though unveiled, in this dark vale, they still
Envelop us, will not let us be free.

WHEN WILL WE START TO LIVE?

When will we start to live? That old refrain,
Reverberating deep within the grain
Of what we are, no matter where or when:

That Siren's Song, so called, or Devil's Trill
Within the will (we think infects the will)
-—Plug up your ears and you will hear it still,

Says life flows out like water through a sieve,
Holds nothing and has nothing much to give,
And leads to nothing: *When will we start to live?*

FRAGMENT OF AN INJUNCTION
TO THE POETS OF THE FUTURE

There is no God. You must begin from that
Presupposition of all modern thought
(Whether or not it recognizes it);
Then you can see what else there is to say.
You must abandon all mythologies,
And in the end accept reality's
Inexorable hold on you, its sway.
No god will hasten you upon the way:
There is no god to guide you or convey—
Nor, for that matter, any Land of Truth
(Such as you may have conjured in your youth)
To which to be conveyed. Forget the myth,
The heroic journey to the Underworld.
The Underworld to which you have been hurled
Is this world—here you are and here it is.
You must abandon all mythologies.

THE AFTERLIFE

The afterlife
Was after life.
There was no life
That was not life.

IN KENSINGTON GARDENS

In Kensington one has one's reveries.
Two river goddesses of polished stone—
They had been waiting through the centuries
And would be there long after you were gone—
Revealed themselves one day in one of these.

TO CARLA, IN LIEU OF THE LOST POEM
I GAVE HER IN HIGH SCHOOL

Those fumblings in your living room—
Afraid your mother would come home.
You never let me go too far,
Wise young virgin that you were:
Always stopped me just before
We'd reached the point of no return.
So every afternoon I'd burn
With longing, which itself was sweet.
It was too soon—we had to wait.
But then too soon it was too late.
For waiting soon became too long
For so much longing—we were young:
Ours was an old, familiar song.

EYELESS IN GAZA

"Eyeless in Gaza at the mill with slaves . . ."
            Milton, *Samson Agonistes*

Eyeless in Gaza at the mill with slaves,
Digging our own and one another's graves,
We have no access to reality.
I blame you, then you in turn blame me.
Subjected to our subjectivity,
We only see the things we want to see.

Eyeless in Gaza, can it be we still
Go round and round that dark, Satanic mill
In vicious circles, playing that old game:
I blame you and then you do the same:
I claim you're a terrorist; you claim
That everything was yours before I came?

I blame, you blame—*I blame you blame me*
Goes on and on in perpetuity.
And blaming becomes bombing in due course,
So *I bomb you bomb me without remorse;*
And in bomb craters we can make our graves—
Eyeless in Gaza at the mill with slaves.

THE FOUNTAIN OF YOUTH

In search of the Fountain of Youth they go
To the beaches of Florida, Mexico,
Or else the Caribbean archipelago:

Old men and women to escape their doom!
Many of my persuasion—those for whom
There is no God or any life to come,
And no Messiah to lead them home.

Fountain of Youth, pure source, hence still unknown,
Sweet bird of youth, once flown, forever gone—
This the conquistador, Ponce de León,
Having sailed to Florida on a galleon,
Discovered for himself and on his own.

THAT ANCIENT HISTORY . . .

That ancient history, those old and stale
Dead metaphors that tell the same dull tale,
Was once again about to envelop us.

It was a chronicle of greed and war—
We'd read the same thing many times before,
And now we too would be inscribed in it.

We thought somehow, in our fatuity,
That we alone were spared—we, only we—
Among the generations of mankind;

And, in our arrogance, that we could spend
Beyond our means, that it would never end:
We had no limits or impediments.

Our dreams were sordid, and these sordid dreams
Were built on monumental Ponzi schemes
That circulated through the ravaged earth.

We all colluded—none of us was pure:
The rich imposed their image on the poor;
The poor had nothing and were envious.

The artists had been neutralized long since:
They were reduced to insignificance
And had no genuine authority;

Nor were there poets to apportion rhymes,
Give weight to words and meaning to the times:
They had no weights or measures, ways or means.

Although we craved only reality,
We had no access other than TV,
The Internet, distractions of that kind—

Gadgets by which to allay our boredom; they
Increased it, didn't make it go away,
And so we looked for new expedients.

Meanwhile the monster Caliban, our crude
Caricature, escaped his chains and spewed
Vituperations on the radio.

Increasingly, we fell beneath the sway
Of repetition, platitude, cliché;
And then our enemies enveloped us.

NOW INDIAN SUMMER . . .

Now Indian summer summons you to take
A long last leave of summer for the sake
Of all the many summers in its wake.

Summing them up, you see that they accrue
Gifts only given to the happy few.
The suns of summer have shone down on you.

Not only sunshine, sometimes also rain;
Pain, but no more than what you could sustain—
All that the Horn of Plenty could contain:

Lovers and friends, relations, children, wives,
The intersections of so many lives,
All with their complicated narratives;

Formidable teachers, Mandelbaum and Fry,
Oppen and Bronk (you hold in memory
Those masters of the art of poetry);

And students, some among them you can say
You left your mark on them in some small way.
You had your work, which also was your play.

You had so much—in nothing were you poor!
Though all the while you always wanted more,
Hungry for life and what life held in store.

The suns of summer, winds of winter came.
Green turned gold, burned by an inner flame,
The cold asserting its eternal claim.

And every year when winter came, it too
Proclaimed the promise of the spring anew.
Proleptically in springtime cold winds blew.

For everything was mixed and joined together!
Sickness and health, joy sadness, pain and pleasure.
There was no measure, knowledge of whence or whither.
Summer and winter circled one another

More and more quickly as the years went by.
More and more rapidly mortality
Bore you along its current to the sea,

Year after year—you tried to hold them fast,
But each one followed hard upon the last,
Falling into the chasm of the past.

Though all the while you knew that this was true,
Year after year an old voice spoke in you:
"Begin again," it said. "Begin anew."

Now Indian summer summons you once more,
More clearly and distinctly than before,
Reverberating from a distant shore.

The yellow leaves of autumn mixed with red,
Brilliant against a blue sky overhead,
Explain what summer meant but never said.

Your task is to interpret what they say,
Record what you have heard while still you may,
Before the winter winds sweep them away.

BEAUTIFUL HOUSES
BUILT OF BRICK AND STONE . . .

Beautiful houses built of brick and stone
Stood on the slope of Westmount Avenue—
In Montreal, the place where I was born.

Even as a child, unknowingly, I knew
They stood for something with solidity,
Something that was self-evidently true.

They spoke the language of civility,
Mellifluously lucid and refined,
Shaped by a concept of nobility

The eighteenth century had redefined,
And on our sad uncertainty conferred
Faith in the destiny of humankind.

I was a child: I spoke and thought and heard
As a child does, unknowingly: the deep
Feelings that habitually were stirred

Within me were inchoate, had no shape,
And would have languished useless and forlorn,
Smothered in silence, swallowed up in sleep,

No sooner born than stifled as if stillborn,
If in that far off time there hadn't been
Beautiful forms to house and give them form,

Till clarity at last should intervene
And consciousness be rendered less obscure.
I was a child: I didn't know it then,

But in this world nothing is ever pure.
No one can ever know another's pain,
And nothing that we value can endure.

Those lovely houses, though they still remain
Standing for values that we thought secure,
In truth will never be raised up again—

We know too much; there's too much to ignore:
The many toiled to build them for the few,
And all their labor only kept them poor.

There wasn't anything that they could do
But follow out the arc of history,
Fulfill their role, then disappear from view.

We know that nothing in the world is free,
And beauty comes at a substantial cost.
The values of the eighteenth century,

With all its universals, have been lost—
Or if not lost, then hedged around by shame,
Resentment and hypocrisy. The ghost

Of poetry still bears that sacred name,
But only lives among the illustrious dead.
I was among the lucky ones: I came

To consciousness after the Muses fled,
But warmed my bones against their dying flame.
Most people lived in poverty and dread.

War, terror, havoc was our constant theme.

SOMETIMES IN CITIES

ꞏ I ꞏ

It seems sometimes in cities that a chance
Encounter quickly blossoms to romance
And life takes on a new intensity.

Two people kiss . . . their senses are renewed,
And happiness, for a brief interlude,
Replaces sacrifice and suffering.

Say that it's make-believe or metaphor . . .
Well, that's what cities actually are for,
Spaces in which to shape our shifting dreams.

So many citizens with hopes and fears,
Who privately pursue their own affairs,
Searching for love and for security.

It seems that cities, paradoxically,
Protect us in our need for privacy,
Letting us cultivate the inner life.

▾   ▾   ▾

Say that these brief encounters do not last—
They have no roots, no purchase on the past,
So usually they wither on the vine.

Often they leave a bitter residue,
As lovely things that vanish tend to do,
Regret or even anguish, guilt and shame.

It may be true; but be it as it may,
It doesn't really matter what we say:
People are driven by the need for love.

—The need for love, transcendence, something new,
Or else the need to hurt themselves—that too!
Or maybe something indeterminate.

All bets are off where Eros is concerned.
Our only knowledge is what we have learned
Skin to skin and through experience.

·II·

It seems sometimes in cities when the rain
At six a.m. beats on the window pane,
You waken to the thought of one you love.

She's far away; you see her in the gloom
Of evening shadows spreading round her room
And wonder what she's feeling, thinking of.

Maybe she's been with friends, or all alone
Has worked all day until the sun's gone down;
Maybe she's also thinking now of you.

It doesn't really matter, but the ache
Of love spreads like a shadow as you wake.
Whatever happens, it will see you through.

·III·

It seems sometimes in cities that the sky
Is unrelenting and the days go by,
Week after week, as if they'd never been:

The heat, humidity, unhealthy air
Externalizing stasis and despair,
The bleak futility you've sealed within.

You ask yourself what else there is to do,
And why it takes you so long to break through,
And whether happiness will come again.

▾ ▾ ▾

She holds you in the moment now; her hand
Holds tight to yours to make you understand
The moment's meaning—not to let it go.

Within the hour you hold her in your bed—
That lovely woman in her desperate need
Whose life holds meaning you desire to know.

Those moments lived within the moment's flow
Will soon be far away and long ago.
You hold those moments in your memory now.

THREE GHAZALS BY RUMI

⋄ I ⋄

What's to be done with religion, dear friends? For I don't know
    myself what to do.
I'm not a Christian, nor yet a Muslim, and certainly not a Jew.

I'm not of the East and not of the West, not born from the sea
    or the earth;
Nor did the circling Heavens beget me, nor Nature preside at
    my birth.

I'm not from the dust, the water, or wind, and not from the
    fire was I sent;
I do not pertain to existence or essence, the ground or the
    firmament.

I am not Indian, Chinese, Russian, nor surely Bulgarian;
I'm not from Iraq and not from Iran, nor yet from Afghanistan.

I'm not of this world, nor yet of the next; I'm neither from Hell
    nor from Heaven;
From Adam and Eve I am not descended, and Eden was never
    my haven.

My place must be placeless, my trace must be traceless; neither
    body nor soul can be.
From the soul of my sole Belovèd I come, from the soul (be it
    He or She).

Having glimpsed the two worlds joining as one, I forgo duality.
It is one that I seek and one that I want, one that I know and
    see.

"For He is the First and He is the Last, the Latent and
    Manifest one."
Besides "O He" and "How great He is," there's nothing that
    can be known.

Now that I've drunk from the cup of Love, I have lost both
    worlds, as you see.
There's nothing that can sustain me now but carousing and
    revelry.

If once in my life I should spend a day without you, I would
    grieve,
Regretting that hour and moment for as long as I might live.

If once in my life I should gain an hour alone with only you,
I'd trample the two worlds under my feet and dance in
    triumph too.

O my belovèd, I'm so drunk, here in this world today:
Aside from drunkenness and revelry, there's nothing I have
    to say.

· II ·

We are the face the mirror reflects and the mirror itself are we.
We are the sober wine cup and wine's drunken revelry.
We are ourselves the cause of pain and the cure for pain are we.
We are the Water of Life as well as the bearer who bears it away.

▾ III

I shut my eyes to creation when I looked upon his face;
Drunk on his grace, forgave myself and gave my own soul grace.

For the sake of Solomon's seal, I was as wax: with all my might,
I polished myself until I gleamed—for the sake of becoming light.

I saw his wisdom and I cast my crooked thoughts away.
I was the reed-pipe on his lips, the plaint that he would play.

I had him in my hands, and yet I blindly sought him out;
And I was in his hands, yet questioned fools who knew him not.

I must have been a fool myself or drunk beyond all measure
That, like a coward, I was stealing that which was my own treasure—

A thief, who through a chink in his own pasture-wall has crept,
Or plucked the jasmine from the very orchard-plot he kept.

Enough! Between your fingers must my secrets always be
Kneaded, or have I twisted in your grasp sufficiently?

Shams-i Tabriz, because of whom the moon and stars give light,
I can see a new moon overhead, though grief has dimmed my sight.

translated by Henry and Paul Weinfield

L'DOR V'DOR:
CHANT OF THE JEWS OF MICHIANA
AS THEY CONTEMPLATE
THE PAST AND THE FUTURE

From generation unto generation
(*L'dor v'dor, l'dor v'dor*),
We were a nation like no other nation:
A scattered, vulnerable population,
We had no land and lived on every shore
(*L'dor v'dor, l'dor v'dor v'dor*).

Amidst hostility and enmity
(*L'dor v'dor, l'dor v'dor*),
Somehow we still kept our integrity,
Our love of ritual and festivity,
Our hold upon futurity therefore
(*L'dor v'dor, l'dor v'dor v'dor*).

Some of us lived in *shtetls* in the Pale
Of Settlement (*l'dor v'dor*).
We worked at various trades—to no avail—
Or earned a meager living from the sale
Of cast-off clothing in a dry goods store
(*L'dor v'dor, l'dor v'dor v'dor*).

We were poor Jews, impoverished but *frumm*
(*L'dor v'dor, l'dor v'dor*),
Living in constant fear of a pogrom,
Not knowing when the Cossacks next would come
To smash the windows and break down the door
(*L'dor v'dor, l'dor v'dor v'dor*).

27

Some of us lived in cities on the Rhine
(*L'dor v'dor, l'dor v'dor*).
Goethe and Schiller were our bread and wine.
We thought the sun was always going to shine
On us and on our children even more
(*L'dor v'dor, l'dor v'dor v'dor*).

We thought that history was on our side
(*L'dor v'dor, l'dor v'dor*).
Modernity, we proudly thought, implied
The universe of Einstein, Marx, and Freud:
Little we knew what history had in store.
(*L'dor v'dor, l'dor v'dor v'dor*).

Six million perished in the Holocaust
(*L'dor v'dor, l'dor v'dor*):
Unnamed numbers, numbered among the lost,
Tossed into pits or gassed, gave up the ghost
In Belzec, Buchenwald, and Sobibor
(*L'dor v'dor, l'dor v'dor v'dor*).

Somebody's sister, mother, cousin, friend
(*L'dor v'dor, l'dor v'dor*),
Came to an end—their lives came to an end.
Something in this we still can't comprehend:
Why did it happen? What was it all for?
(*L'dor v'dor, l'dor v'dor v'dor*).

Those who survived, who rose up from the dead
(*L'dor v'dor, l'dor v'dor*),
Bewildered and benumbed with grief and dread,
Now came to where the fortunate had fled—
Those who had managed to escape before
The horror had commenced (*l'dor v'dor*).

And some among these sad remaining few
(*L'dor v'dor, l'dor v'dor*)
Came to a land where oranges now grew.
They learned an ancient language, now made new,
But found here too the constant threat of war
(*L'dor v'dor, l'dor v'dor v'dor*).

Others among them happened to be hurled
(*L'dor v'dor, l'dor v'dor*)
Hither and yon and all across the world.
In the Americas their lives unfurled—
In Canada, Brazil, and Ecuador
(*L'dor v'dor, l'dor v'dor v'dor*).

O my America, you rescued these
Most wretched immigrants (*l'dor v'dor*):
You were a refuge for these refugees.
And they, in turn, they and their families,
Enriched your life in ways one can't ignore.
(*L'dor v'dor, l'dor v'dor v'dor*).

Now they were joined to that same steady flow
Of co-religionists (*l'dor v'dor*)
Who had come recently or long ago—
Whom poverty and prejudice made throw
Their fates to the four winds and thus explore
A brave new world (*l'dor v'dor v'dor*).

Through Ellis Island's port of entry came
Most of these passengers (*l'dor v'dor*).
And if a Yiddish-speaker, asked his name,
Should answer "*Sheyn fargesn!*" that became
"Sean Ferguson"—the name he henceforth bore
(*L'dor v'dor, l'dor v'dor v'dor*).

Most of us settled in the Lower-East
Side's broken tenements (*l'dor v'dor*).
Thereafter, as our numbers were increased,
To Brooklyn and the Bronx we were released
And spread along the Eastern corridor
(*L'dor v'dor, l'dor v'dor v'dor*).

Thence to Detroit, Chicago did we wend
Our way (*l'dor v'dor, l'dor v'dor*);
Then, turning south, we reached our journey's end—
The towns of Mishawaka and South Bend
Along the Saint Joseph River's winding shore
(*L'dor v'dor, l'dor v'dor v'dor*).

In 1857 we arrived
(*L'dor v'dor, l'dor v'dor*).
We founded schools and synagogues (they thrived)
And cemeteries, where our mourners grieved—
The institutions at our very core
(*L'dor v'dor, l'dor v'dor v'dor*).

We put down roots, dug deep, and life went on
(*L'dor v'dor, l'dor v'dor*).
We did what we habitually had done
In all times, since our wanderings were begun
With Abraham, our ancient ancestor
(*L'dor v'dor, l'dor v'dor v'dor*).

Here in the American heartland—the Midwest
(*L'dor v'dor, l'dor v'dor*),
We cherished life, grew prosperous, were blessed,
Acknowledging the presence of the past
And wondering what the future has in store
(*L'dor v'dor, l'dor v'dor v'dor*).

PARADISE LOST: A POEM
IN TWELVE BOOKS:
THE SHORTER VERSION

"None ever wished it longer than it is."
        Samuel Johnson, "The Life of Milton"

". . . the troublesome and modern bondage of Riming."
        Milton, "Note to 'The Verse'"

BOOK
˙ I ˙

Satan awakens in the depths of Hell
With those of his compeers who also fell:
Moloch invoked and Mammon, Belial,
And many more (the rest were long to tell).

BOOK
˙ II ˙

After a consultation they agree
On Satan's plan: to thwart the deity
He'll bring destruction on humanity.
First, meeting Sin and Death, his progeny,
Satan through Chaos wings upon his way.

BOOK
ᐧIIIᐧ

Meanwhile in Heaven the Almighty looking down
Upon our two first parents from his throne
Turns to address his only begotten Son.
They locked in mutual admiration
Are both agreed that nothing can be done;
For Man will hearken to the evil one.
Yet, taking on Man's sin as if his own,
The Son, incarnate, brings redemption
Through his own death and resurrection.
But now the Adversary, all alone,
Alighting on the World's most outer zone,
Finds passage to the orbit of the Sun,
Sees Uriel, but managing to shun
Him, makes his way to Mount Niphates soon.

BOOK
▾ IV ▾

Satan in prospect now of Paradise,
Assumes a cormorant's shape, and in that guise
Flies to the Tree of Life, there to devise
Evil and death for all mankind. He spies
Adam and Eve in bliss, taking their ease,
And pines with longing at the sight he sees,
Then leaves to explore Eden's peripheries.
Now came still evening on, and night. Eve lies
With Adam, sated by love's ecstasies,
In innocence, and innocently wise,
When Satan to their bower in secret hies.
Unto her ear the evil one applies
A dream, in hopes that evil might arise.
Discovered by the angelic guards, he flees.

BOOK
▾V▾

Eve when she wakes is racked with chilling fear.
She pours her dream into her husband's ear.
He clears her doubts, and yet a silent tear
Falls from each eye—she wipes them with her hair.
So all is cleared (but not completely clear).
God, to ensure that those in Eden hear
The prohibition dire and persevere
In their obedience, sends an angel there.
Eve makes him lunch—they dine on earthly fare
(Angels have bodies: do not live on air).
The angel Raphael recounts how ere
The World was made, God hastened to declare
Upon a day, his Son and only heir
Had been begotten—angering Lucifer
(Satan henceforth), who raised up many a peer,
But was opposed by Abdiel's zeal severe.

BOOK
ᵥVIᵥ

All night the Seraph Abdiel, unafraid,
Through Heaven's wide champaign his long journey made.
Unto the seat supreme he was conveyed
With high applause—from whence a mild voice said,
"Servant of God, well hast thou done, indeed."
Now were the armies in their ranks arrayed.
Abdiel struck Satan: though his spear upstayed
Him, he recoiled, which made the angels glad.
His trumpet sounded, Michael raised his blade
And with swift wheel reverse deep entering flayed
Satan's right side. The devils were dismayed
To see the nectarous stream that Satan bled;
Yet soon he healed, for spirits, even bad,
Can never die—unless they are unmade.
The devils now bring cannon to their aid,
A triple-mounted row of pillars laid
On wheels, which when the angels saw displayed
They heaved up mountains at their foes. God bade
His Son bring closure to the whole charade,
And from his strong right arm the devils fled,
Hurling themselves to Hell in utmost dread.

BOOK
⸳VII⸳

To Adam, at his request, is now related
How and wherefore this world was first created:
After the rebel angels were defeated,
With Heaven's population much depleted,
God sends his Son, in glory unabated,
To fashion a new world (all this was fated).
Six days elapse before the consecrated
Labor of Creation is completed.
With alleluias it is celebrated.
The Son ascends to Heaven—retranslated.

BOOK
˙VIII˙

Adam implores the angel to make clear
Whether the stars are rolled around Earth's sphere
Or Earth rolls round the Sun (as some aver).
"Dream not of other worlds, what creatures there
Live, in what state," replies the angelic seer:
"Leave them to God above; him serve and fear."
Adam, thus cleared of doubt and anxious care,
Tells how he came awake (though unaware
Of who he was, or from what cause, or where),
And how he found within himself the power
Of naming things. "From where I first drew air,
On a green bank profuse with many a flower,
One came, methought, of shape divine, who bore
Me to the garden he had readied here.
His heavenly did my earthly overpower:
Dazzled and spent, sunk down, I sought repair
Of sleep, which swiftly fell on me. The glor-
ious shape opened my side: from thence he tore
A rib with cordial spirits, streaming gore
(Wide was the wound, but seemed itself to cure).
Under his hands a creature he did rear,
Manlike, but different sex, so lovely fair
That sweetness came to my heart, unfelt before.
She left me dark. I waked to search for her—
To find her or forever to deplore
Her loss, and other pleasures all abjure—
When out of hope, behold her, not gone far:
Brought by her Heavenly Maker, she drew near.
I led her blushing to the nuptial bower."

The affable archangel cries: "Beware!"

38

BOOK
· IX ·

Satan involved in rising mist is veiled;
Then in the wily snake he lies concealed—
The Serpent, subtlest beast of all the field.

Now when the Earth with sacred light was filled,
Adam and Eve go forth, as God had willed,
To tend the Garden tending now to wild.

The Garden's wanton growth seemed to deride
The hands' dispatch of two gardening so wide,
And thus to urge their labors to divide.

For both these gardeners, though innately skilled,
Had only rudimentary tools to wield,
By which to cultivate what lay untilled.

"Let us divide our labors!" Eve appealed
To Adam thus; he, being much assailed,
Against his judgment felt compelled to yield.

▾　▾　▾　▾　▾

Surging toward Eve the circling Serpent rolled,
Fold upon fold, a maze of verdant gold.
He was a lovely Serpent to behold.

His tongue was tuned and intricately trolled
Flattery, as her beauty he extolled.
His song was sung, his story duly told.

Eve, in that story, having now grown bold,
No longer wishing to remain controlled,
In evil hour reaches out, takes hold,
And eats the fruit that brought death to the World.

Adam, astonished, feels his veins run cold,
But he too eats, encouraged and cajoled.
Earth feels the wound, Nature is unconsoled,
Mourns innocence, and, giving birth, grows old.

BOOK
ᐧ X ᐧ

Now with the Sun in western cadence low,
Came the mild Judge and Intercessor too
To sentence Man. To Eve he said in few:
"Say, woman, what is this which thou didst do?"
She answered sadly—what she said was true.
Because he couldn't punish Satan, who
Had made the Serpent instrument of our woe,
He said, "Because thou hast done this, cursed art thou:
Upon thy belly groveling thou shalt go.
Eve's seed will hold thee ever as his foe:
He'll bruise thy head, and thou his heel also."
"Thy sorrow," to the woman he said now,
"With thy conception I will cause to grow.
Bringing forth children thou shalt undergo
Labor, and to thy husband's will shalt bow."
On Adam last pronounced he judgment. "Know:
Cursed is the ground for thy sake: thou in sorrow
Shalt eat thereof from morrow unto morrow
Through all thy days, and reap what thou didst sow.
Thistles and thorns for thee the earth shall spew.
Bread thou shalt eat in the salt sweat of thy brow—
Till thou return unto the ground, for lo!
Dust thou art and shalt return thereto.

ᐧ   ᐧ   ᐧ   ᐧ   ᐧ

Meanwhile Sin and Death, to make the way
Easier to cross, construct a broad highway
From Hell to this World over Chaos. They
Encounter Satan hastening to relay
What he accomplished in his earthly stay.
—He and the devils will be made to pay
By being turned to serpents (for a day
Or two each year—or so, at least, some say);
But Sin and Death are free—the World's their prey!
Over all beasts, birds, plants they now hold sway.
The scythe of Time mows all things, come what may.
Fish, flesh, and fowl return unto their clay.
All are now mortal, subject to decay.

▾   ▾   ▾   ▾   ▾

From his transcendent seat the Almighty sees
These Hell-hounds, Sin and Death, as now they seize
And lay waste to the World—lands, skies, and seas.
"Man's folly let these Furies in," he says,
"Who think me foolish that with so much ease
I gratify my scornful enemies.
I drew them hither to lick up the lees
And filth, which human sin, spreading disease
To what was pure, in all things now displays,
Till crammed with glutted offal they appease
Themselves with gorging at the end of days,
And at one sling of thy strong arm, well-pleas-
ing Son, through Chaos hurled, obstruct and freeze
The mouth of Hell, and seal his ravenous jaws.
Then Heaven and Earth, purged of impurities,

Shall be renewed in sanctity. On these,
Till then, the curse that has been uttered stays."
He ended, and the heavenly Audience raise
Loud alleluias to intone his praise:
"Who can extenuate thee? Just are thy ways.
On all thy works righteous are thy decrees."

BOOK
▾XI▾

Thus they repentant stand in lowliest plight.
Prevenient grace had made their hearts contrite,
And winged their prayers to Heaven with speediest flight,
But Nature's law no longer will permit
Them to retain their Garden of delight.
Michael is sent to lead them out of it
(They bitterly lament but must submit),
But first takes Adam up unto a height,
With euphrasy and rue purging his sight,
Where he can see what future things await.
The initial vision he must contemplate
Is of his own son Abel's dreadful fate
As victim of his brother's murderous hate.
He is shown ways too numerous to cite
That evil comes to blot out or to blight
The lives of suffering humans soon or late—
Because of Man's ungoverned appetite,
And emanating from the fruit Eve ate.
A bevy of fair women, richly dight,
He next is shown, who wantonly incite
The men that, eyeing them, are ravished quite.
Just men, they seemed, and bent on doing right,
But in the net are caught. In amorous heat
These Sons of God and Daughters of Men unite,
And Hymen! Hymen! sounds the marriage rite.
From thence arose the Giants of great might,
Men of renown who glory in the fight—
In violent acts that violent acts requite.
One eminent in wise deport, a white-

haired man, in opposition rose to indict
Their crimes: him had they seized upon to smite,
Had not a cloud shrouded him from their spite,
And raised him up unto the heavenly light.

▾　　▾　　▾　　▾　　▾

He looks, and sees the clouds turn black, and rain
Battering the Earth till nothing can be seen.
Amidst that desolate and dismal scene,
All are consumed—plants, animals, and men.
Only an ark floats on the watery main.

But when at last the storm begins to wane,
The ark hull sticks on mountainous terrain;
A raven, as the waters start to drain,
Flies from the ark; then once, and yet again,
A dove goes forth to spy out something green.
An olive leaf he brings, pacific sign.

Dry ground appears on mountain and on plain.
The ancient sire descends with all his train.
Above his head he sees a cloud wherein
A colored bow is sign that though Man sin,
God never more will seek to have him slain,
Or drown the World and every beast with Man—
Till fire purge all things new and justice reign.

BOOK
▾ XII ▾

After the Angel Michael has explained
What following the Flood has been ordained—
Especially how the promised seed will mend
The things that have been broken—they descend
The Hill of Speculation, to attend
On Eve, who waking from a dream has gained
The understanding Adam has obtained.
But now too nigh, in bright array, a band
Of Cherubim descend, in front the brand-
ished Sword of God ablaze, to desert sand
Turning that temperate, once fertile land.
Michael takes hold of both our parents, and
Leads them direct to Eden's eastern bound-
ary, then down the cliff and to the plain beyond—
Then disappears, no longer to be found.
They looking back, all the eastern boundary scanned,
Waved over by the gate, that flaming brand,
With dreadful faces thronging all around.
The World was all before them—nothing planned:
With wandering steps and slow, they hand in hand
Through Eden took their way alone. *The End*

·II·

THREE ACADEMIC ADDRESSES

FOOD FOR THOUGHT

Now that we all have dined on earthly fare
(Though "fair," I fear, is going rather far),
We'll feed on delicacies beyond compare
In an impromptu Great Books Seminar.

I'll let you choose the text because I'm kind.
No more than six or seven hundred pages
For Friday morning's class will be assigned.
—Books should be read in manageable stages.

An after-dinner treat, to aid digestion,
Might be a portion from *Of Cannibals*.
Or chew on Aristotle: my suggestion
Would be Book I of *Parts of Animals*.

Or how about a sermon from Augustine:
Perhaps the passage where he steals some pears?
Forbidden fruit is really quite disgustin',
But people tend to want what isn't theirs.

Malthus's *Principles of Population*
Might give those planning families some pause . . .
Why not a little *Tusculan Disputation*
Or extract from the *Peloponnesian Wars*?

Let's see what Buddha or old Lao Tzu,
Those Oriental sages, have to say.
It doesn't really matter what we do,
Since everything is *maya* anyway.

I like the Greeks, but some prefer the Persians:
We read, or feed, according to our taste;
We all have inclinations and aversions—
De gustibus non disputandum est.

Professor Crowe likes ham but isn't taken
With even the finest cut Virginia Woolf;
Professor Bartky cannot stomach Bacon;
I'm not too fond of anything Freud myself.

Professor Munzel, as a steady diet,
Can feed on Kant's sublimities for weeks!
The *Prolegomena* . . . she'd have you try it
As antipasto to the three *Critiques.*
But Nietzsche and Wittgenstein and Heidegger
Are somewhat less palatable to her.

Professor Fallon's *Samson* grows ever stronger—
"Eyeless in Gaza . . ."—what a lovely line!
But nobody ever wished it any longer—
I'm sorry if that sounds too Philistine.

Leviathan and *Moby Dick*: a feast
For those of us who happen to like whale;
But Jonah in the belly of the beast
Is how those monsters sometimes make me feel.

Devouring books, we are ourselves devoured—
A cautionary note therein is rung.
How to escape, without becoming soured,
The *enantiodromia* discerned by Jung?

Left to itself, thought festers, soon grows specious,
And man descends to nothingness—as shown
By Darwin, Shakespeare, Sophocles, Lucretius:
We cannot thrive on any one food alone.

This is the reason, though our lives are hectic,
We turn our knowledge on the ancient wheel.
Competing wisdoms hone our dialectic;
They teach us how to reason and to feel.

We must have Plato, then, at our symposium—
But nothing from Books two or three or ten
Of *The Republic*, where, *ad nauseam*,
Poets are made to take it on the chin.

Philosophers have hated us since Plato—
It sometimes seems they've nothing else to do;
And every hectoring moralist, like Cato
In Dante's *Purgatorio*, canto two,
Considers it consonant with his position
To relegate a Virgil to perdition.

Forgive me if intrudes some bitterness
On what should be a jovial occasion.
We all have our pet peeves in PLS,
Which makes for our "eternal conversation."
And given the vicissitudes of history,
It's not surprising if we disagree.

Like Marx—not Karl; it's Groucho that I cite—
I sometimes wouldn't want to be included
In any sort of company that might
Include me (present company excluded).
And even if he invited me, I'd say,
"I'm sorry, Plato: Thank you, anyway.

"I've hitched my broken wagon to the West,
Laden with books, all heaped up in a jumble:
It's not Utopia, but we do our best.
With luck, with humor, maybe if we're humble,
We'll find at least we recognize the road.
I have to go now—while the going's good."

APOSTROPHES

Monday and Wednesday afternoon
We meet in seminar; the hours
Pass quickly, are no longer ours:
Already February is gone.
Meanwhile Melissa Flores flowers:
She's going to have a baby soon.

Maybe the baby she will bear
Will write as beautifully as Flaubert
Or Dostoevsky; maybe he—
Or she—like Marx or Freud, will be
The harbinger of something new,
Someone who tells us what is true.
If truth's a woman, she gives birth
And thus replenishes the earth,
And making all things new is born
Herself successively in turn.
This is what Nietzsche helps us see
As we confront modernity;
It's not what Plato thought, or Kant,
But in the end is what we want.

If it's a boy I hope she names
Him something else than William James.
That's far too boring! Fyodor,
Dmitri, Alyosha, or
Ivan or Smerdyakov will do
Much better—to suggest a few.
Let's hope, if it's a boy, he'll be

Like Alyosha, not his three
Brothers; let's hope that one day he
Has Grushenka sit upon his knee
(I'm fond of her myself, you see).
Let's hope, if it's endowed with ovaries,
Her life won't be like Madame Bovary's.

The term is only half-way through:
We've got a lot of work to do!
There still are many books to read,
Each one of which could be the seed
Inseminating what you are
And bearing you up to your own star—
Far from our Great Books Seminar.
Meanwhile, we hope, before too long
(Maybe before we get to Jung)
Melissa Flores will give birth
To someone new upon the earth—
A little baby girl or boy
Searching instinctively for joy,
And from its earliest infancy
Struggling unconsciously
For meaning and for what may give
Purpose to the life we live.
This is a never-ending quest.
But may this girl or boy be blessed
In childhood and throughout its youth
With books that seek to explore the truth—
Books that teach us to revere
The life we live in common here:
This is our hope and this our prayer.

THE SEMINAR

Reading, we are embedded in the text:
We don't remember who or where we are.
The leaves are turning—one leaf, then the next:
The years are passing in the seminar.
Its seeds disseminated near and far
Are thoughts that slowly ripen in the sun.
Some have grown old and some are new begun
When thirty years have vanished—who knows where?

The great Achilles rises from the mists—
We see him striding through the asphodel.
He is a shade, yet somehow he exists:
He tells us what the shades alone can tell,
They who once lived but now in Hades dwell.
And silently he bids us recognize
The golden sunshine and the spacious skies
As blue as on the morning that he fell.

Then Diotima talks to us of love,
How giving birth in beauty is its goal.
Beauty, she says, is radiant above
All of the other objects of the soul;
And so we hunger for the beautiful,
Our mortal share in immortality.
It lifts us up beyond the things we see,
Till what we see is beauty as a whole.

Devote your study to the way things are,
Lucretius says; for what else can you do?
Though grim Religion and relentless War
Assail mankind, Venus will see you through.
Nothing will come of nothing (yes, it's true:
Lucretius said it long before King Lear);
And death is nothing—nothing at all to you,
Because when you are dead you won't be there.
Therefore, my children, be ye of good cheer!

But Anselm argues irrefutably
In the *Proslogion* that God cannot
Be thought not to exist; for God, you see,
Is that than which no greater can be thought.
If God did not exist (as we've been taught),
It follows as a consequence there'd be
Something that one could think of greater than He—
And that's a contradiction, is it not?

All shall be well, and all things shall be well.
Dame Julian of Norwich makes this claim.
And though we fail, and though in failing fell,
Our gracious Lord imputes to us no blame.
When he, the ground of our beseeching, came,
It was to share in our humanity.
What Julian was shown appeals to me,
And it would be my own theology,
If I were not the heathen that I am.

A man is born along the Indus: he
Has never heard of Christ, but even so,
He lives a life of virtue, decency.
Where is this justice that consigns him to
Perdition? Dante asks; and even though
The Eagle answers him equivocally
In *Paradiso*, canto nineteen, the
Question will resonate incessantly;
The problem that it opens up will grow.

What do I know? in his *Apology*
Montaigne will ask; and for the Renaissance
This opens up epistemology.
He knew that if he had been born by chance
Along the Indus River, not in France,
He'd have thought differently. Contingency
Conditions us to who knows what degree.
Experience confirms our ignorance.

Montaigne engenders Descartes and Pascal,
Both of whom seize upon the Absolute.
They don't want partial truth—they want it all.
Reason is radical, goes to the root,
But sometimes leaves the flower and the fruit
To wither on the vine or fail to grow.
The heart has reasons reason doesn't know,
But, failing to communicate, is mute.

Spirit and flesh, habitual enemies,
Are reconciled, as in a radiant dream,
In Mozart's captivating melodies.
And though those old antinomies still scheme
To heap blame on the hero—blame and shame—
However much they thrust him to perdition,
The music raises him to its condition.
The sensuous is its essential theme.

The real is rational in Hegel's view
And reason is made known in history.
Somehow I've never found this to be true.
That history's the struggle to be free
Is, on the contrary, no mystery.
If the World-Spirit really has a plan,
I hope that it will show it, if it can,
And that it's one with which I can agree.

Minerva's Owl at evening takes flight
As shadows lengthen on modernity.
The waning sun no longer gives much light,
And it's becoming harder now to see
The path that leads us to futurity.
In this dark wood, how shall we make our way?
How much do Marx and Nietzsche have to say?
Our metaphysics has been stripped away.
Is *active love* our only certainty?

Civilization and its discontents
Weigh heavily as the generations pass.
For some, the canon merely represents
A pantomime of gender, race, and class.
The concept of humanity, alas,
Increasingly seems harder to uphold.
Even our ironies have now grown old.
Our public speech has never seemed so crass.

So be it, then; of this we can be sure:
That which we love is that which will remain.
Only the books we cherish will endure;
So we must cherish them: so be it, then.
The patterns they impose, expose, contain
Our contradictions and complexities.
In this dark wood, commune among the trees.
Read and reread and read them all again.

·III·

FROM OLD NOTEBOOKS

SONNET

All night I heard the ringing of a bell,
And saw the pages turning of a book.
I was in Hell (I knew that this was Hell)—
But then I was awakened by the clock.
Your friend and I, both of us still in shock,
Drove in the dark to where your body lay,
Filling the emptiness with idle talk
Until the blackness of the night turned gray.
Your widow waited for us at the door,
Black with a blackness I had never seen.
The blackness wasn't in the clothes she wore,
But in her anger, in her very skin.
You took your life, and hers, she must have known,
Would be no more than gray from that time on.

1981; 2017

GEORGE OPPEN'S EYES

The eyes that looked out from your photograph
Were sad but sane—a human being's eyes.
They'd seen how humans suffer, how they laugh
At others' suffering, and how they lie.
Among the poets, yours were the only eyes
That never dimmed themselves in fantasies,
Or looked to compromise the poet's craft
Out of a vain desire to be heard.
The only motive for your poetry
Was *clarity*, you said, your favorite word.
I looked upon you as another father,
And hoped I might find favor in your eyes.

1984; 2018

TO ONE DYING OF LEUKEMIA
IN SALT LAKE CITY

You lie in bed in the hospital;
    Your wife sits by your side.
The camera is fixed on the window-sill;
    Its lens is open wide.
A microphone intones your name,
And tells your story and whence you came.

Twenty years ago, an enlisted man,
    You saw the bombs explode.
With greater force than the bombs of Japan,
    They fell near where you stood—
So near that with your eyelids closed
You could see the bones of your hands exposed.

The Army had an "exercise"
    To measure the extent
Of "troop-emplacement casualties,"
    And you were its instrument.
This exercise assuaged its fears,
For you have lived for twenty years.

A man can live a normal life
    For twenty years, maybe:
Work at a job, marry a wife,
    And raise a family;
Nor dream that though his life be good,
Leukemia devours his blood.

But poets and physicians know
　　That there are hidden laws,
And that the evil worm may grow
　　Without apparent cause,
Till unbeknownst, by slow degrees,
It spreads a hundred maladies.

Both poets and physicians deem
　　From what these laws impart
That things are never what they seem—
　　Hence physic and hence art.
Both poets and physicians tell
That things are metaphysical.

But lacking their experience,
　　The Army does not find
The "proof of concrete evidence"—
　　To all else being blind.
And what the Army does not see,
It says is not nor cannot be.

Petitions to the government,
　　The government denied.
The case is without precedent;
　　The courts must hence decide
Whether the effects of radiation
Shall constitute an obligation.

For all this process still proceeds!
    And after you have died,
Your widow in her widow's weeds,
    Who now sits by your side,
Shall plead for such as she might claim
By way of stipend in your name.

A man of simple dignity,
    To bitter death resigned,
You do not curse the obliquity,
    Which nothing can rescind,
The affliction of humanity;
For you are a man and you must die.

A man of true nobility,
    To death being reconciled,
Your last responsibility
    Is to protect the child
In whom you further and renew
The hopes that were cut off in you.

This is the reason you allowed
    The cameras in to see
What otherwise you'd have been too proud.
    This was your strategy,
Your sole defense in dealing with
The bureaucratic monolith.

It may be that the story ends
    In the usual comedy
With the Army moved to make amends
    To avoid the hue and cry,
And Congress sponsoring a bill—
Such things are not impossible.

The poet stands outside your door—
    He cannot heal the sick.
The body is a metaphor,
    The body politic,
Where if in one a cancer dwells
It gnaws the nation's vital cells.

The poet stands outside your room—
    He sees that he cannot see
Whether in twenty years to come,
    In twenty years, maybe,
Nothing of man but his disease
Shall live to chant his obsequies.

But you have given the poet faith,
    And he shall not forbear
To praise the courage which in death
    You transmit through the air;
For something is which does not stop,
And while we breathe we still must hope.

1978; 2019

LIKE SISYPHUS, LIKE TANTALUS

Like Sisyphus, you heave the boulder,
The weight of failure on your shoulder,
And it grows heavier as you grow older.

Like Tantalus in his despair,
You reach for grapes that are not there—
Or when you grasp them, disappear.

Fearing it always will be thus,
You seek surcease—a terminus—
Like Sisyphus, like Tantalus.

1978; 2019

SPLEEN

Charles Baudelaire

I'm like the king of a rainy and cold
Country, but powerless, young but so old,
Who scorning the tutors who do his behests,
Is bored with his dogs as with all other beasts.
Nothing can cheer him, not hunting nor falconry,
Nor the people dying in front of his balcony.
The grotesque ballad of his favorite fool
Can't serve to distract any longer this cruel
Sick man, nor the ladies-in-waiting for whom
All princes are handsome—his bed is a tomb.
No matter how lewd the attire they don,
They can't crack a smile from this young skeleton.
Nor yet can the *savant* who makes him his gold
Withdraw the corruption that rots in his soul.
And even these blood-baths, a legacy of Rome,
Which rulers recall when their last days come,
Can't warm his cadaver, where red blood flows never,
But only the waters of Lethe's green river.

1979; 2019

·IV·

WHEN THE DARK DAYS COME

THE BALLAD OF DONALD TRUMP

Now, for our sins, there comes a man named Trump
Running for president. He's on the stump,
Playing whoever listens for a chump.

America, he'll make you great again!
This is his slogan, this is his refrain.
He's going to rid you of your *angst*, your pain,
This snake-oil salesman, glib American.

His language is the language of cliché,
He wears what seems to be a blonde toupee,
He has a lot of debts but doesn't pay,
And what his tax bill is, no one can say.

He says he's going to build a wall so wide
That aliens will never get inside
Our borders (if they do, they'll have to hide).

No Mexican will ever get the notion
Of sneaking in and causing a commotion.
No Syrian will dare to cross the ocean.

Trump's Tower of Babel, we shall call it, high
Above our heads will dominate the sky,
Arresting those that creep or swim or fly.

As for the Chinese he will make a deal
That brings that nation's multitudes to heel.
The trade pacts that we signed he will repeal
And steal the jobs that other nations steal

From us. He's going to do it, we can guess,
By paying workers fifty cents or less
An hour, so the jobs now shipped offshore
Won't go to Bangladesh or Singapore.
We'll make the t-shirts that our workers buy
At Walmart's over here. It's worth a try!

He milked his companies and had to fend
Off bankruptcy six times, but in the end
He stiffed his own suppliers and didn't bend.
The money that was his he didn't spend.
Vladimir Putin is his dearest friend.

The walls of his apartment, we've been told,
Are lined with gold—twenty-four carat gold.
Small wonder that our leaders have been sold
To lobbyists, whose interests they uphold;
For most are cast out of the self-same mold.

Two hundred and thirty thousand dollars for
A wedding dress that trailed along the floor . . .
She wore it once—will never wear it more.
(No need to add: it might have fed the poor.)

He says that climate change is just a hoax,
One of those fraudulent, malicious jokes
That scientists inflict on common folks.

Resist their war on coal! And by the way,
Our weapons of assault are here to stay
(That's one thing they will never take away).
As patriots who love the U.S.A.,
We pledge allegiance to the N.R.A.

He is a master of exaggeration,
Which sadly seems compelling to a nation
That only wants to vent its indignation.

No doubt its anger is well justified.
Imagine all the soldiers that have died
Only because some politician lied.

After the housing bubble finally burst,
The Ponzi-scheming bankers were the first
To cash their chips in and ride out the worst.
But ordinary people were immersed
In debt, they lost their jobs, their lives seemed cursed.

Now, unsurprisingly, they feel forgotten.
They yearn for change, they think the system's rotten.
They want a *Strongman*. Here is what they've gotten:

A veteran of Reality TV,
The founder of a university,
A populist whose popularity,
Untainted by the least vulgarity,
Is based on kindly acts of charity

(In the old days he kept the indigent
   Out of his buildings—who knows where they went?
   "Black welfare cheats" who wouldn't pay the rent),
A paragon, indeed, of probity
   (When Scottish homeowners refused to sell
   Their properties to him, he built a wall
   To block their ocean view—and that's not all:
   To pay for it, he had them sent the bill),
Whose wealth and power suit him to a tee.

Out of whatever depths of guilt or shame,
Prepared by history, this monster came,
Now that he's come, he comes to stake his claim.

One thing is clear: we've made ourselves a mess.
The damage isn't easy to assess.
How it will end is anybody's guess.

VILLAINELLE

What goes around, soon comes around again.
If you cause pain, pain will accrue to you,
And be repeated like an old refrain.

You moved the embassy and now complain
The Palestinians dropped the other shoe?
What goes around, soon comes around again.

One hardly needs to have an Einstein's brain
To ascertain that what's been said is true.
It's been repeated like an old refrain.

This song was sung in Portugal and Spain
By exiled Muslim and by exiled Jew.
What goes around, soon comes around again.

In Poland it was certainly made plain,
And now in Syria they sing it too.
It's been repeated like an old refrain.

We have a President who is insane.
Nobody knows what he will say or do.
What goes around, soon comes around again,
And is repeated like an old refrain.

WHEN THE DARK DAYS COME

When the dark days come, how will you fare?
Will you be sunk in torpor and despair,
To which so many at the end succumb,
And, as your body comes undone, grow numb,
Anxiously waiting when the dark days come?

When the dark days come, what will remain?
Will everything you've done seem done in vain,
And pain be passage to oblivion?
What of your wife, your daughters, and your son?
What will you leave them when the dark days come?

When the dark days come, as come they shall,
For neither hopes nor wishes can forestall
Them, will you seize on any fallen crumb,
Blind to the consequences, deaf and dumb?
What will you stoop to when the dark days come?

When the dark days come, and like a wave
Break heavily upon you, will you grieve,
Happy though you have been beneath the sun,
For what was done and what was left undone,
Uselessly longing when the dark days come?

You who have lived your life as in a dream,
Drunk on appearances, on how things seem,
Always addicted to delirium:
What did you mean? What meanings did you glean?
Who will it turn out then that you have been,
After the sands have summed their final sum?
What will you answer when the dark days come?

AS THE CROW FLIES

Late afternoons when the light dies,
Crows rise into the bare winter skies.
At evening we can hear their raucous cries.

If you could look into a crow's black eyes,
Would what you found make you foolish or wise?
Would you take a crooked path and go on telling lies,
Or finally go straight—as the crow flies?

ABOUT THE AUTHOR

 HENRY WEINFIELD's most recent collections of poetry are *Without Mythologies: New and Selected Poems and Translations* (2008) and *A Wandering Aramaean: Passover Poems and Translations* (2012)—both with Dos Madres. In 2019, Dos Madres published his translation of *The Chimeras* by Gérard de Nerval, with illustrations by Douglas Kinsey. His other verse-translations include versions of the *Collected Poems of Stéphane Mallarmé* (1994), Hesiod's *Theogony and Works and Days* (2006; done in collaboration with Catherine Schlegel), and *The Labyrinth of Love: Selected Sonnets and Other Poems* by Pierre de Ronsard, forthcoming from Parlor Press. Weinfield is also the author of *The Poet without a Name: Gray's Elegy and the Problem of History* (1991), *The Music of Thought in the Poetry of George Oppen and William Bronk* (2009), and *The Blank-Verse Tradition from Milton to Stevens: Freethinking and the Crisis of Modernity* (2012). He is the editor of William Bronk's *Selected Poems* (1995) and *From the Vast and Versal Lexicon: Selected Poems by Allen Mandelbaum* (2018). He is Professor Emeritus of Liberal Studies and English at the University of Notre Dame.

Other books by Henry Weinfield
published by Dos Madres Press

The Tears of the Muses (2005)
Without Mythologies (2008)
A Wandering Aramaean (2012)
The Chimeras by Gérard Nerval
(translation) (2019)

He is also included in:
Realms of the Mothers:
The First Decade of Dos Madres Press - 2016

For the full Dos Madres Press catalog:
www.dosmadres.com